ORANGE YOU GLAD?

A KNOCK-KNOCK JOKE IN RHYTHM AND RHYME

By BLAKE HOENA

Illustrated by KLAUS BIPPER

Music Arranged and Produced by MUSICAL YOUTH PRODUCTIONS

CANTATA
LEARNING

WWW.CANTATALEARNING.COM

CANTATA
LEARNING

Published by Cantata Learning
1710 Roe Crest Drive
North Mankato, MN 56003
www.cantatalearning.com

A note to educators and librarians from the publisher: Cantata Learning has provided the following data to assist in book processing and suggested use of Cantata Learning product.

Publisher's Cataloging-in-Publication Data
Prepared by Librarian Consultant: Ann-Marie Begnaud
Library of Congress Control Number: 2015958178
    Orange You Glad? : A Knock-Knock Joke in Rhythm and Rhyme
    Series: Jokes and Jingles
    By Blake Hoena
    Illustrated by Klaus Bipper
    Summary: Rhythmic music is paired with a graphic novel format to tell this classic knock-knock joke.
    ISBN: 978-1-63290-596-3 (library binding/CD)
    ISBN: 978-1-63290-639-7 (paperback/CD)
Suggested Dewey and Subject Headings:
    Dewey: E 818.602
    LCSH Subject Headings: Fruit – Juvenile humor. Fruit – Songs and music – Texts. Fruit – Juvenile sound recordings.
    Sears Subject Headings: Jokes. | Food – humor. | School songbooks. | Children's songs. | Jazz music.
    BISAC Subject Headings: JUVENILE NONFICTION / Humor / Jokes & Riddles. | JUVENILE NONFICTION / Music / Songbooks. | JUVENILE NONFICTION / Cooking & Food.

Book design and art direction, Tim Palin Creative
Editorial direction, Flat Sole Studio
Music direction, Elizabeth Draper
Music arranged and produced by Musical Youth Productions

Printed in the United States of America in North Mankato, Minnesota.
072016   0335CGF16

When we get hungry between meals, it's **snack** time! But it's not always easy finding a treat that is both **healthy** and tasty. That is especially true for Susie Loo. In her kitchen, there's a pesky fruit knocking on the **cupboard** door and rapping on the refrigerator.

To find out who's there, turn the page and sing along!

Oh, Susie Loo was looking for a snack
when from the kitchen cupboard,
she heard a rap-ity rap.

So Susie Loo kept looking for her snack,
and from the refrigerator
there came a tap-ity tap.

Oh, Susie Loo wasn't sure what to do,
when she reached for a drawer
and heard a boom-ity boom.

Orange you glad I didn't say banana!
Banana! Banana-nana-nana!
Banana! Banana! Banana-nana-nana!
Banana! Banana! Banana!

Susie Loo was **annoyed** and ran away.

She hid in her bedroom, but

there came a clang-ity clang.

Out of her room and down the hall she sprang,
but the knocking followed her,
with a loud bang-ity bang.

Little Susie ran outside in her socks.
She climbed into her **tree house**.
Still, there was a knock–ity knock.

18

SONG LYRICS
Orange You Glad?

Oh, Susie Loo was looking for a snack
when from the kitchen cupboard,
she heard a rap-ity rap.

Knock! Knock!
Who's there?
Banana.

I don't want a banana!

So Susie Loo kept looking for her
   snack,
and from the refrigerator
there came a tap-ity tap.

Knock! Knock!
Who's there?
Banana.

I said no bananas!

Oh, Susie Loo wasn't sure what to do,
when she reached for a drawer
and heard a boom-ity boom.

Knock! Knock!
Who's there?
Orange.
Orange who?

Orange you glad I didn't say banana!
Banana! Banana-nana-nana!
Banana! Banana! Banana-nana-nana!
Banana! Banana! Banana!

Orange you glad I didn't say banana!
Banana! Banana-nana-nana!
Banana! Banana! Banana-nana-nana!
Banana! Banana! Banana!

Susie Loo was annoyed and ran away.
She hid in her bedroom, but
there came a clang-ity clang.

Knock! Knock!
Who's there?
Banana.

Please, no more bananas!

Out of her room and down the hall
   she sprang,
but the knocking followed her,
with a loud bang-ity bang.

Knock! Knock!
Who's there?
Banana.

Arg! No bananas!

Little Susie ran outside in her socks.
She climbed into her tree house.
Still, there was a knock-ity knock.

Knock! Knock!
Who's there?
Orange.
Orange who?

Orange you glad I didn't say banana!
Banana! Banana-nana-nana!
Banana! Banana! Banana-nana-nana!
Banana! Banana! Banana!

Orange you glad I didn't say banana!
Banana! Banana-nana-nana!
Banana! Banana! Banana-nana-nana!
Banana! Banana! Banana!

But I *really* like oranges.

Orange You Glad?

Jazz
Musical Youth Productions

Verse

1. Oh, Su - sie Loo was look - ing for a snack when from the kitch - en cup - board, she heard a rap - i - ty rap.

Knock! Knock! Who's there? Ba - na - na. I don't want a ba - na - na!

Verse 2

So Susie Loo kept looking for her snack,
and from the refrigerator there came a tap-ity tap.
Knock! Knock! Who's there?
Banana. I said no bananas!

Pre Chorus

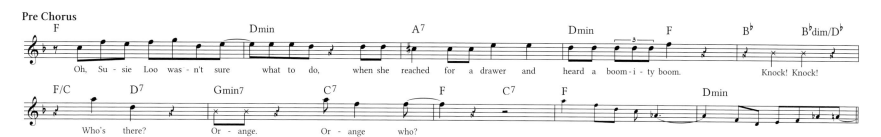

Oh, Su - sie Loo was - n't sure what to do, when she reached for a drawer and heard a boom - i - ty boom. Knock! Knock!

Who's there? Or - ange. Or - ange who?

Chorus

Orange you glad I did - n't say ba - na - na! Ba - na - na! Ba - na - na - na - na - na - na - na! Ba -

na - na! Ba - na - na! Ba - na - na - na - na - na - na! Ba - na - na! Ba - na - na! Ba - na - na!

Verse 3

Susie Loo was annoyed and ran away.
She hid in her bedroom, but there came a clang-ity clang.
Knock! Knock! Who's there?
Banana. Please, no more bananas!

Verse 4

Out of her room and down the hall she sprang,
but the knocking followed her, with a loud bang-ity bang.
Knock! Knock! Who's there?
Banana. Arg! No bananas!

Pre Chorus

Little Susie ran outside in her socks.
She climbed into her tree house. Still, there was a knock-ity knock.
Knock! Knock! Who's there?
Orange. Orange who?

Chorus (x2)

Outro

But I real - ly like or - ang - es.

GLOSSARY

annoyed—made to feel angry

cupboard—a cabinet for storing dishes or food

healthy—something that is good for you

snack—a small amount of food to eat between regular meals

tree house—a playhouse built in a tree

GUIDED READING ACTIVITIES

1. In this story, Susie Loo is looking for a snack. Can you remember what kind of fruit she likes? What kinds of snacks do you like?

2. What is your favorite fruit? The banana in this story could sing and dance. Draw a picture of your favorite fruit singing and dancing.

3. Susie Loo runs outside to get away from the banana. Where does she go? Do you have a place you like to go when you are upset or annoyed? Where is it?

TO LEARN MORE

Baltazar, Art. *Welcome to the Treehouse*. North Mankato, MN: Stone Arch Books, 2013.

Cornell, Kari A. *Awesome Snacks and Appetizers*. Minneapolis: Millbrook Press, 2014.

Lee, Sally. *Healthy Snacks, Healthy You!* Mankato, MN: Capstone Press, 2012.

Segarra, Mercedes. *Yummy Snacks: Little Chef Recipes*. Berkeley Heights, NJ: Enslow Elementary, 2014.